If I Were an Angel...

Lee Ann B. Marino, Ph.D., D.Min., D.D.

If I Were an Angel…

Lee Ann B Marino, Ph.D., D.Min., D.D.

Published by:
Burning Bush Books
(An imprint of The Righteous Pen Publications Group)
www.righteouspenpublications.com

Book classification:
1. Juvenile Nonfiction > Religions > Christianity>General.

ISBN: 1-940197-74-0
13-Digit: 978-1-940197-74-6

Printed in the United States of America.

Be ye not forgetful
to entertain strangers:
for thereby some have
entertained angels unawares.
(Hebrews 13:2)

FOR THE GROWN-UPS

Many children have questions about angels that are often hard to answer. Given we don't often hear much about angels except during the Christmas season, it's very possible answering a child's question about what angels look like, what they do, where they are, and why we have them may prove challenging. It can be difficult to simplify spiritual things as a rule, and angels are no exception. We see many examples of angelic work throughout Scripture, with them serving as divine messengers, comforters, protectors, warriors, guides, friends, encouragers, and companions, with each situation and circumstance a little different from the others.

Written in a moment of inspiration nearly twenty years prior to publication, *If I Were an Angel...* seeks to explain the work of angels in a fun and easy-to-read rhyming manner for children. Serving as a first primer for interest in angelology, this text is complete with Bible passages throughout that relate in some way to the rhyme as well as angelic education. Not seeking to deviate from Scriptural insight, I do acknowledge taking some poetic license to describe the different things angels do to provide practical illustration of their work. Designed to be both educational and entertaining, this book also contains illustrations of angelic encounters throughout history – from Renaissance artwork to post-Victorian imagery.

As a minister and educator for twenty-five years at the time of publication, it is my greatest hope this book can answer the questions and spark intrigue of the special child in your life who desires to explore the ways that all that is both seen and unseen sometimes overlap through God's special messengers known as angels.

Dr. Lee Ann B. Marino, Ph.D., D.Min., D.D.
Author

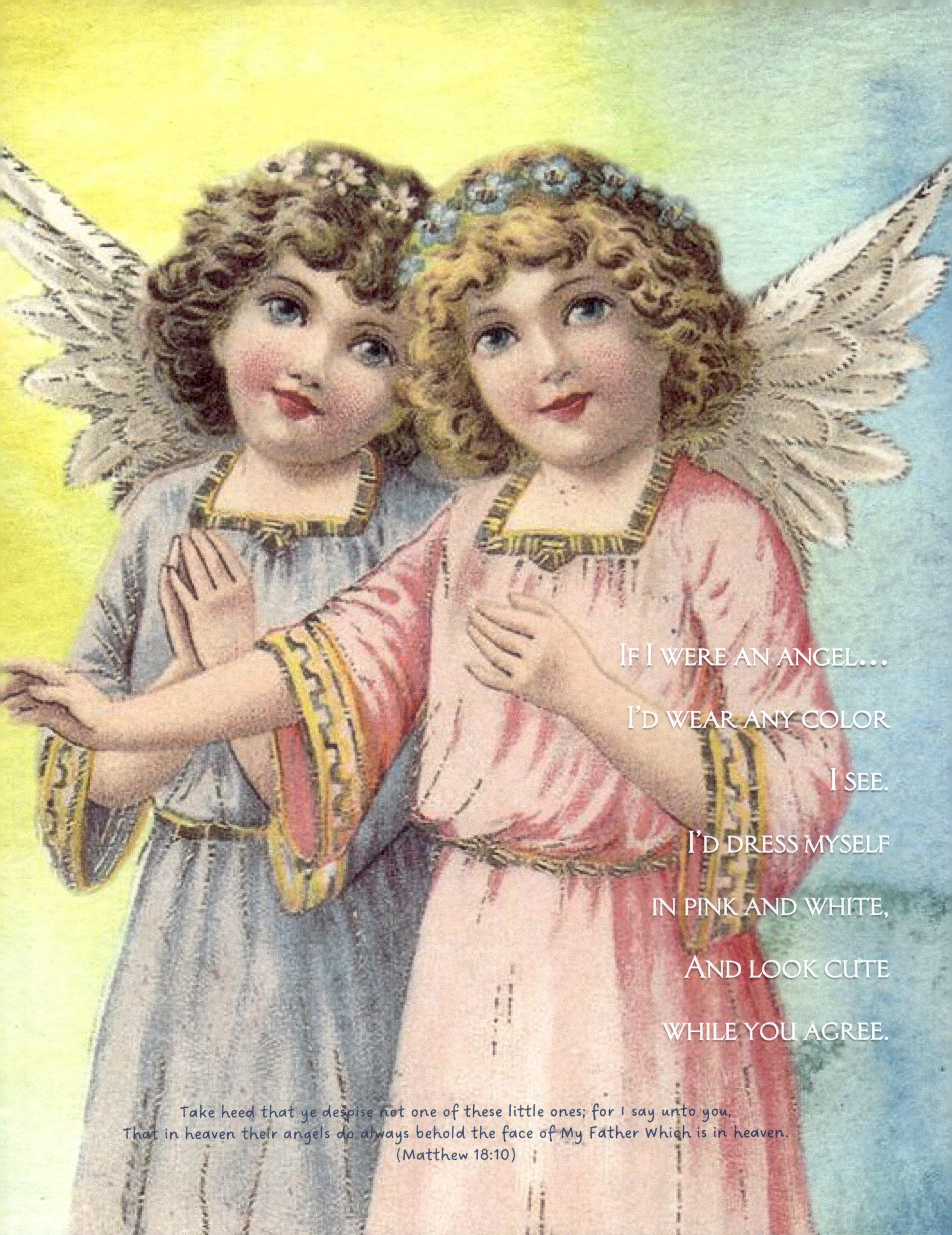
If I were an angel…
I'd wear any color
I see.
I'd dress myself
in pink and white,
And look cute
while you agree.
Take heed that ye despise not one of these little ones; for I say unto you,
That in heaven their angels do always behold the face of My Father Which is in heaven.
(Matthew 18:10)

If I were an angel…

I'd have pretty wings;

And sing a song

of joy and peace,

That tells of

spiritual things.

And the seven angels which had the seven trumpets prepared themselves to sound.
(Revelation 8:6)

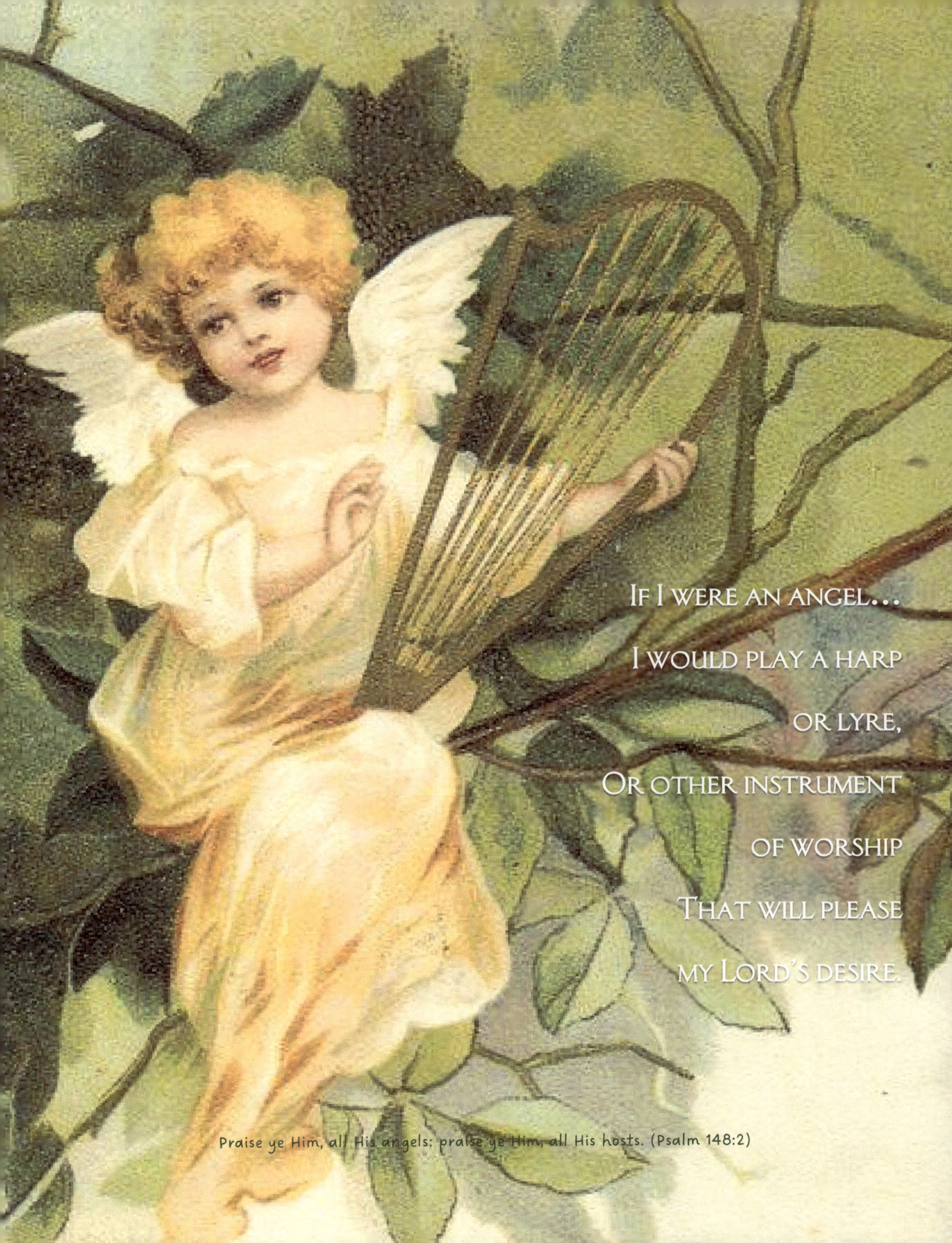
If I were an angel…
I would play a harp
or lyre,
Or other instrument
of worship
That will please
my Lord's desire.
Praise ye Him, all His angels: praise ye Him, all His hosts. (Psalm 148:2)

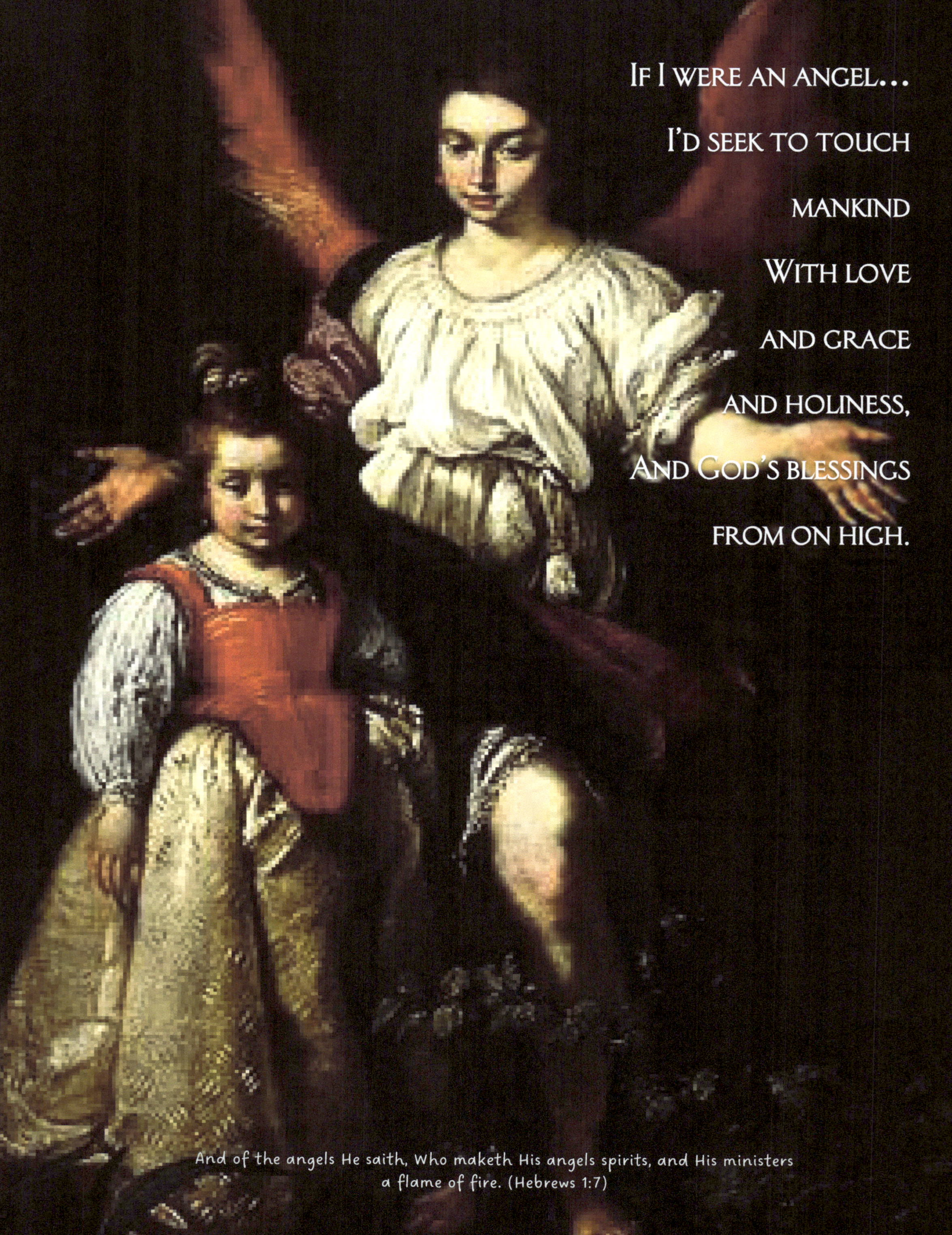
If I were an angel…
I'd seek to touch
mankind
With love
and grace
and holiness,
And God's blessings
from on high.
And of the angels He saith, Who maketh His angels spirits, and His ministers
a flame of fire. (Hebrews 1:7)

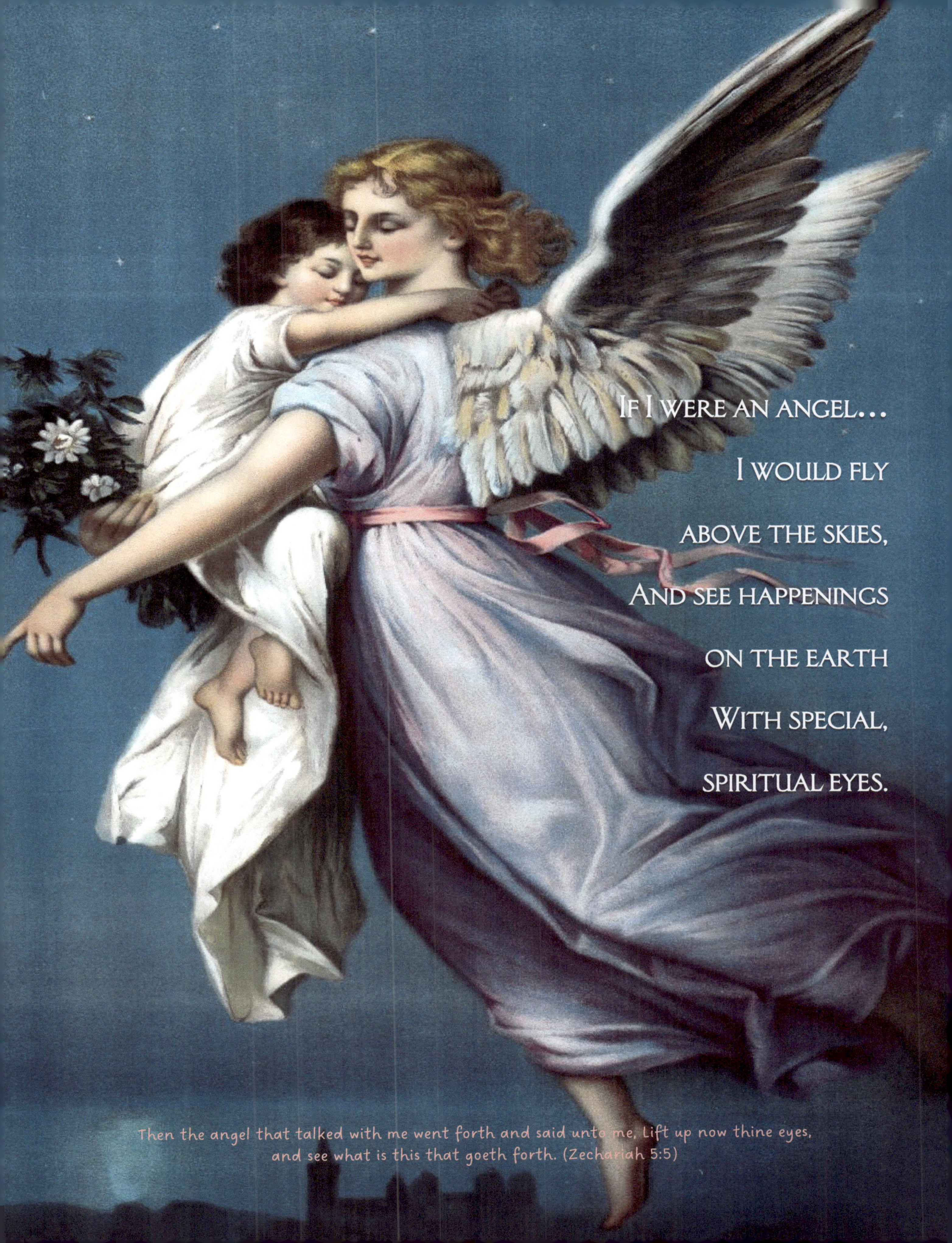

If I were an angel…

I would fly

above the skies,

And see happenings

on the earth

With special,

spiritual eyes.

Then the angel that talked with me went forth and said unto me, Lift up now thine eyes, and see what is this that goeth forth. (Zechariah 5:5)

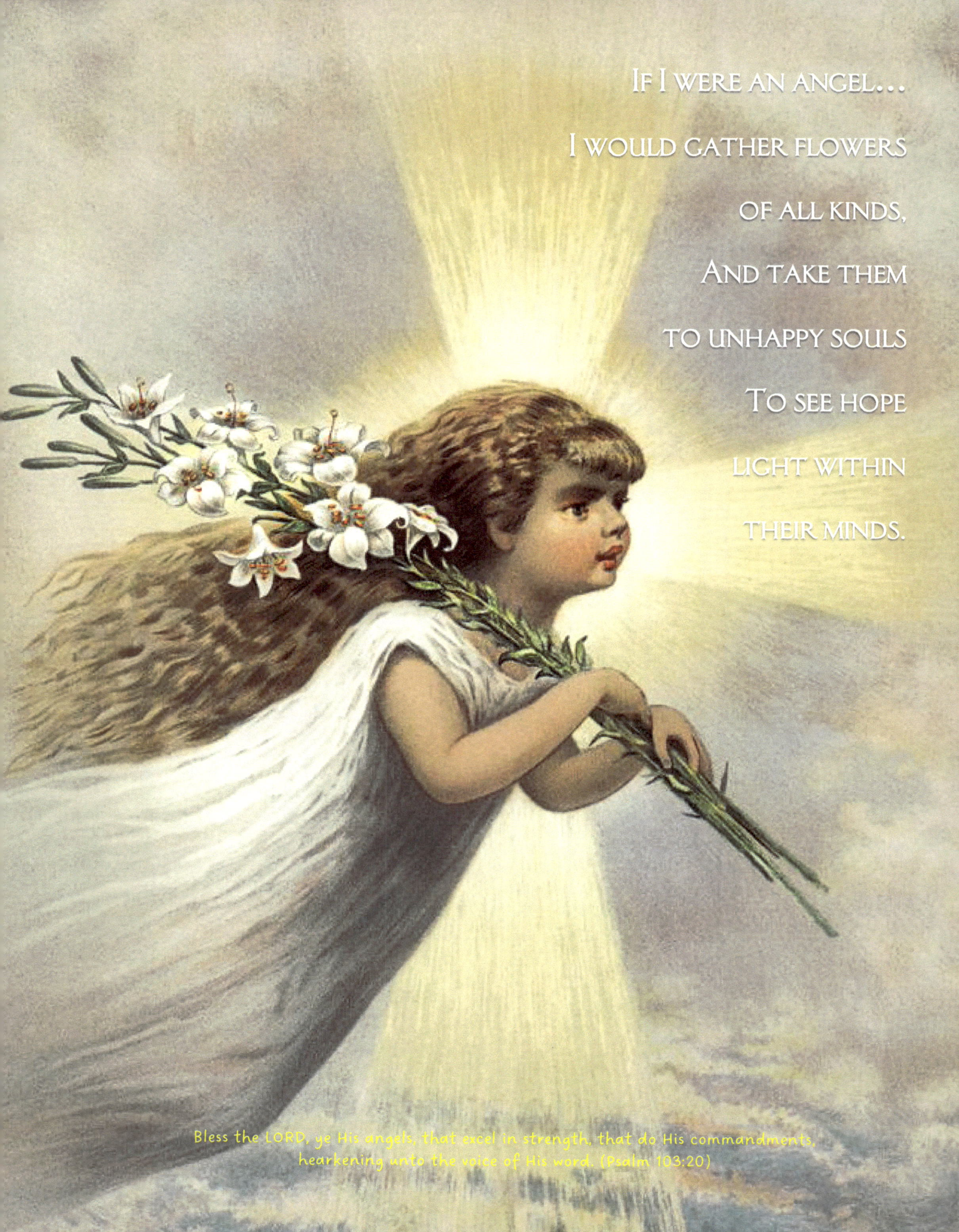
If I were an angel…
I would gather flowers
of all kinds,
And take them
to unhappy souls
To see hope
light within
their minds.
Bless the LORD, ye His angels, that excel in strength, that do His commandments,
hearkening unto the voice of His word. (Psalm 103:20)

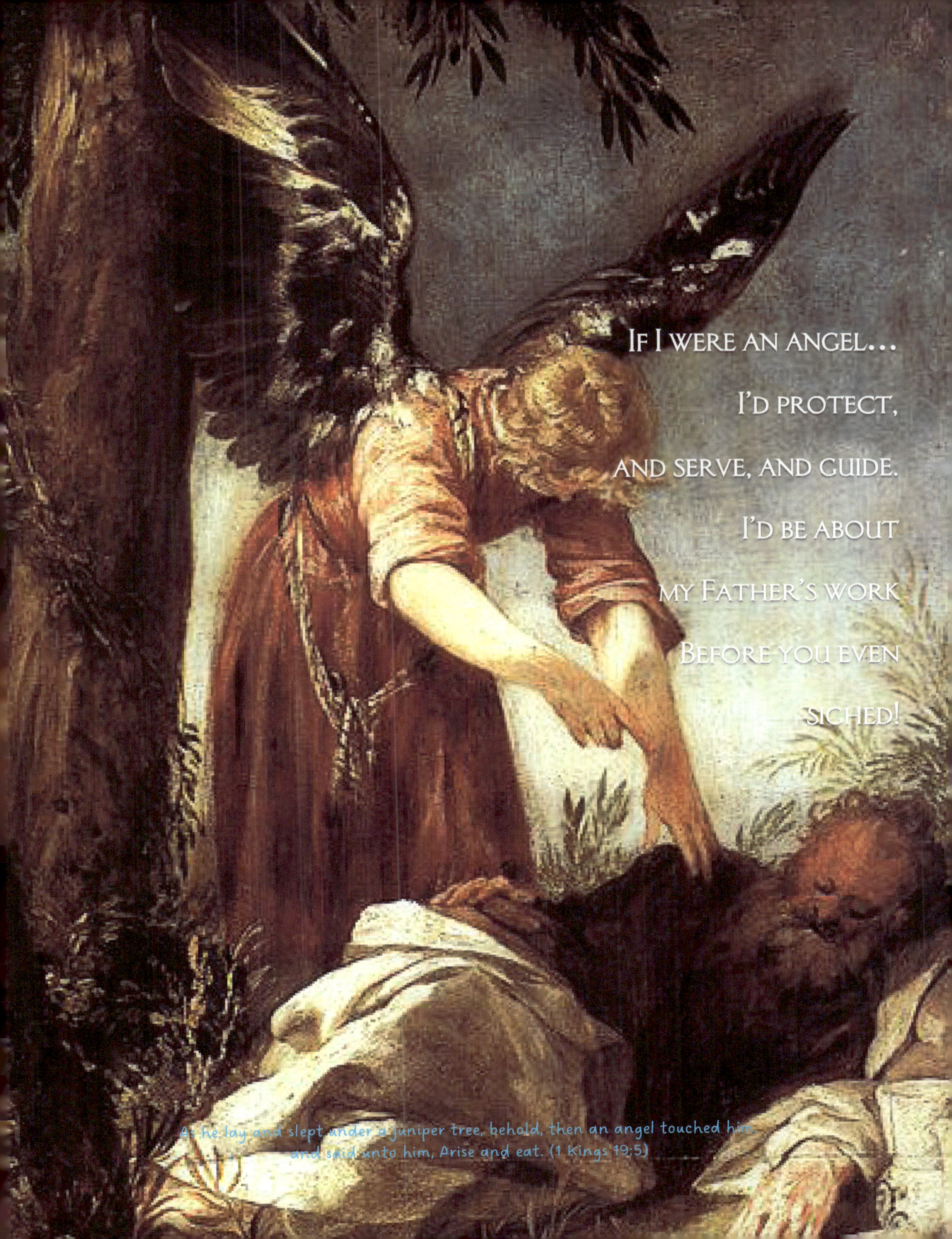
If I were an angel…
I'd protect,
and serve, and guide.
I'd be about
my Father's work
before you even
sighed!
As he lay and slept under a juniper tree, behold, then an angel touched him,
and said unto him, Arise and eat. (1 Kings 19:5)

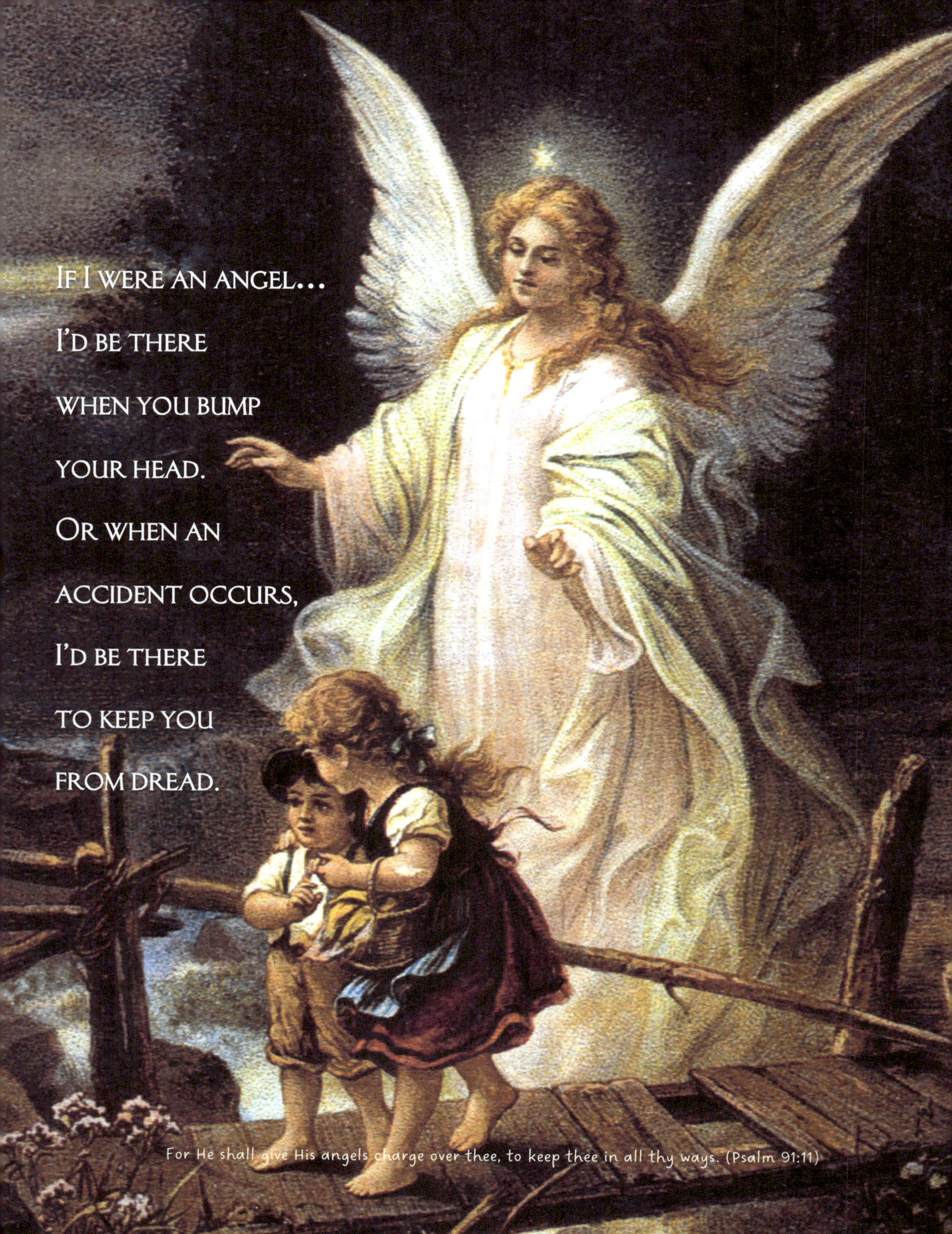
If I were an angel…
I'd be there
when you bump
your head.
Or when an
accident occurs,
I'd be there
to keep you
from dread.
For He shall give His angels charge over thee, to keep thee in all thy ways. (Psalm 91:11)

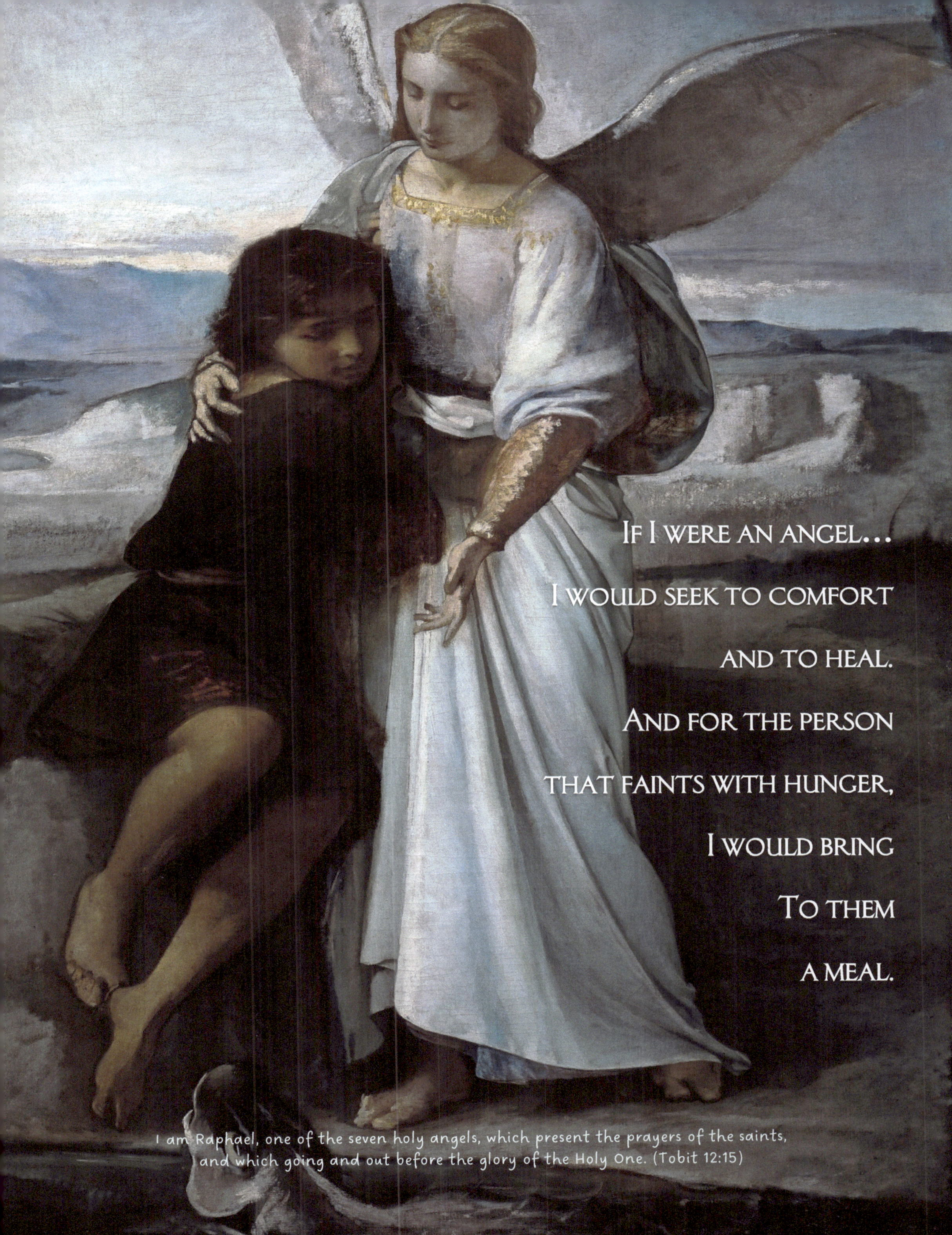
If I were an angel…
I would seek to comfort
and to heal.
And for the person
that faints with hunger,
I would bring
To them
a meal.
I am Raphael, one of the seven holy angels, which present the prayers of the saints,
and which going and out before the glory of the Holy One. (Tobit 12:15)

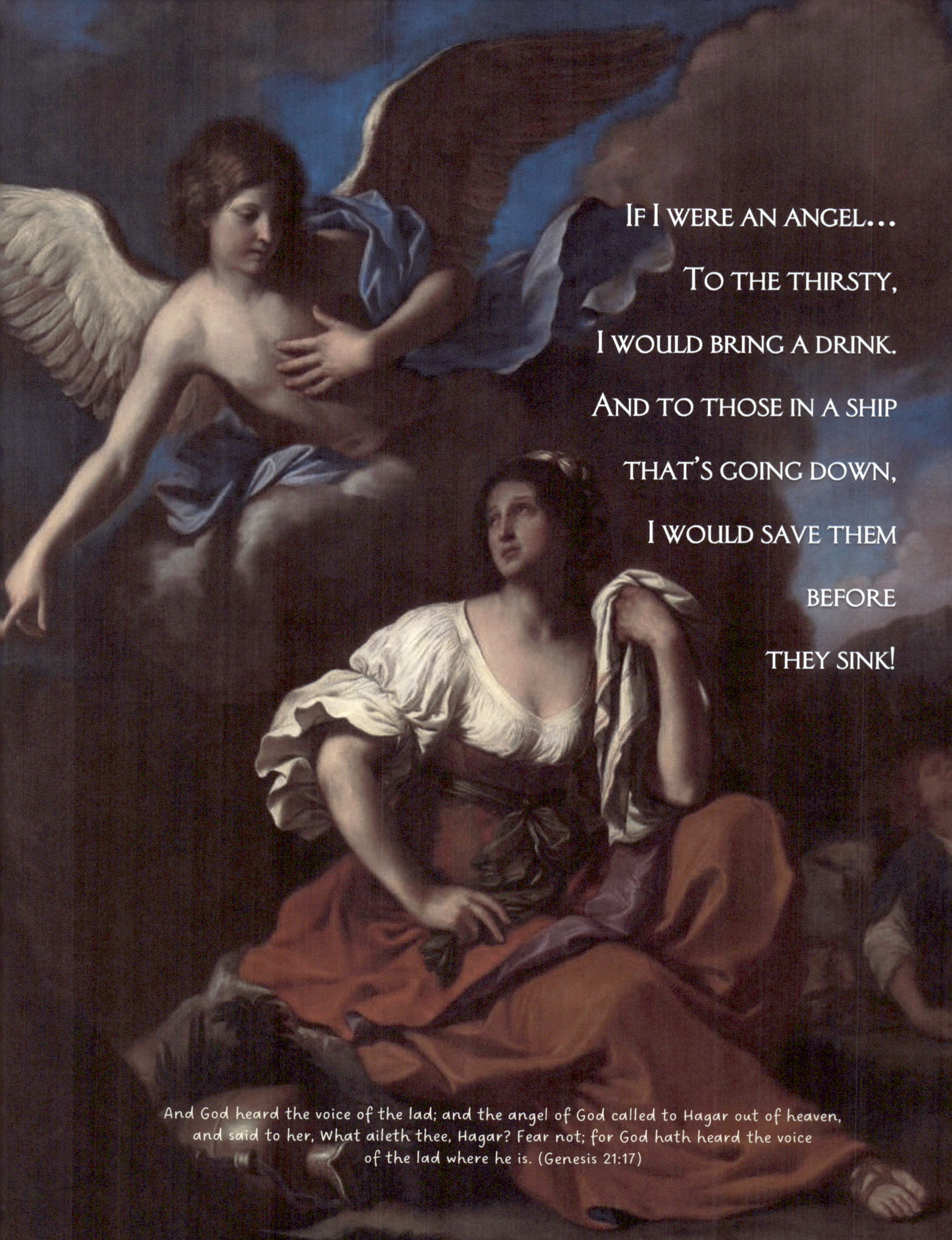
If I were an angel…
To the thirsty,
I would bring a drink.
And to those in a ship
that's going down,
I would save them
before
they sink!
And God heard the voice of the lad; and the angel of God called to Hagar out of heaven, and said to her, What aileth thee, Hagar? Fear not; for God hath heard the voice of the lad where he is. (Genesis 21:17)

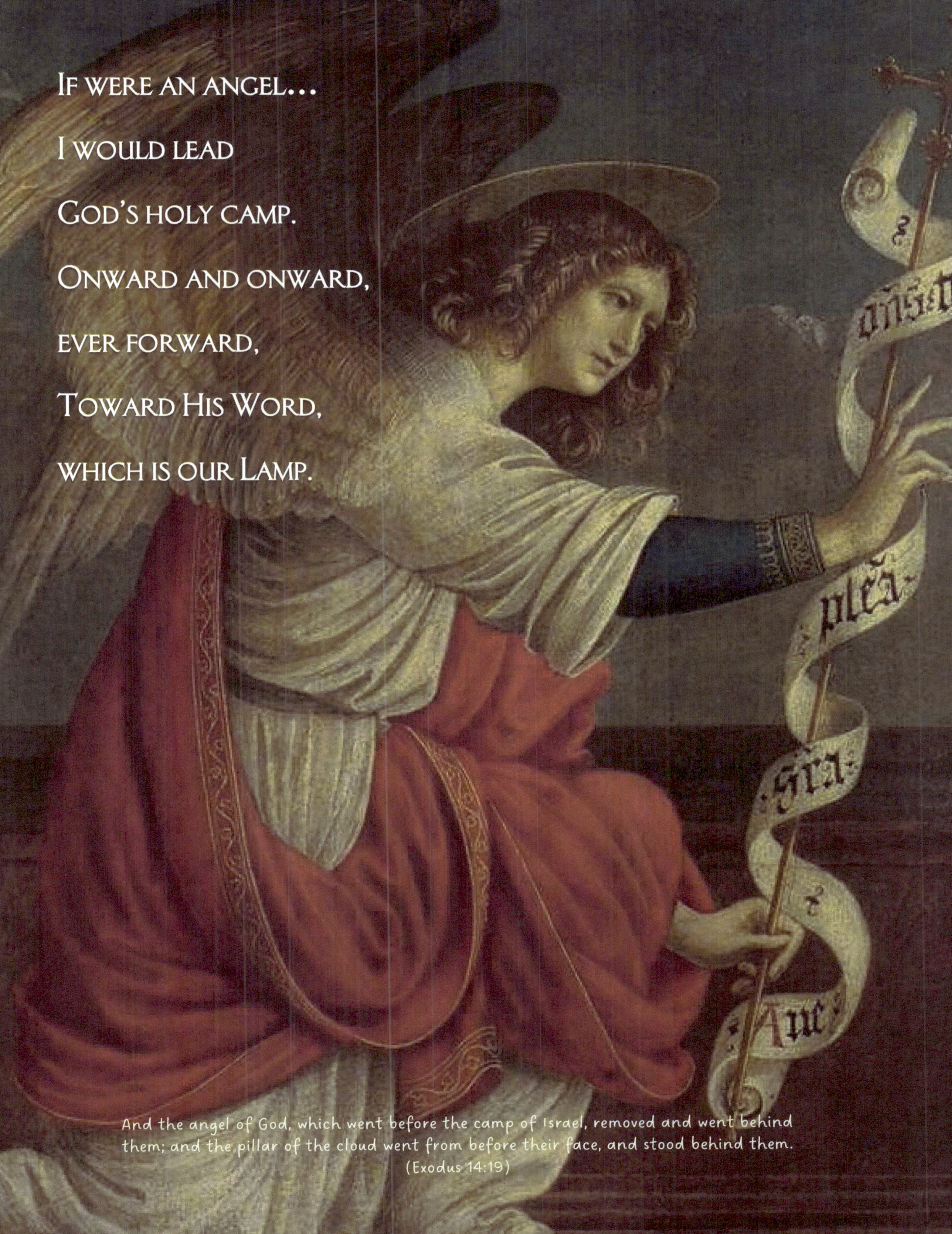

If were an angel…

I would lead

God's holy camp.

Onward and onward,

ever forward,

Toward His Word,

which is our Lamp.

And the angel of God, which went before the camp of Israel, removed and went behind them; and the pillar of the cloud went from before their face, and stood behind them.
(Exodus 14:19)

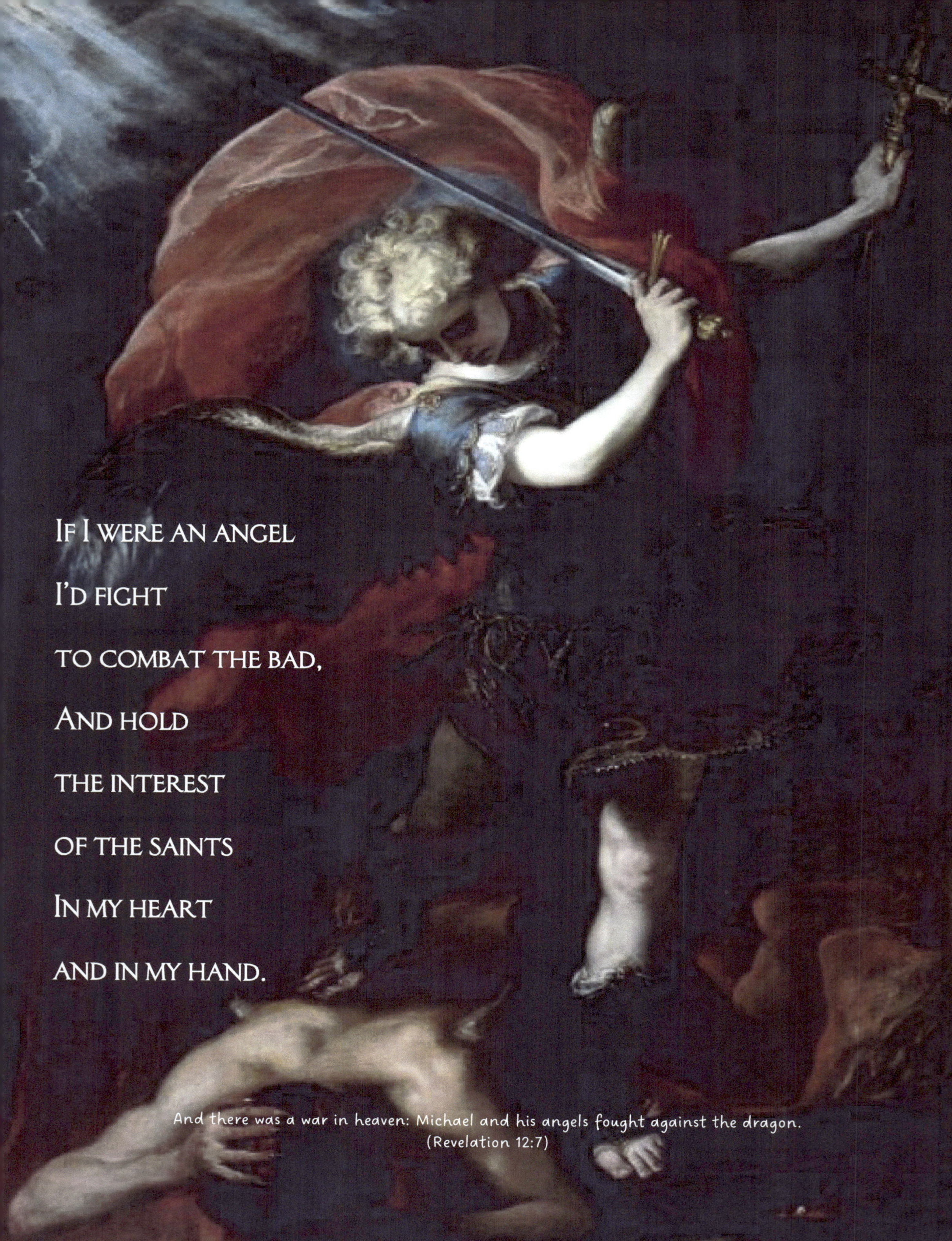

If I were an angel
I'd fight
to combat the bad,
And hold
the interest
of the saints
In my heart
and in my hand.

And there was a war in heaven: Michael and his angels fought against the dragon.
(Revelation 12:7)

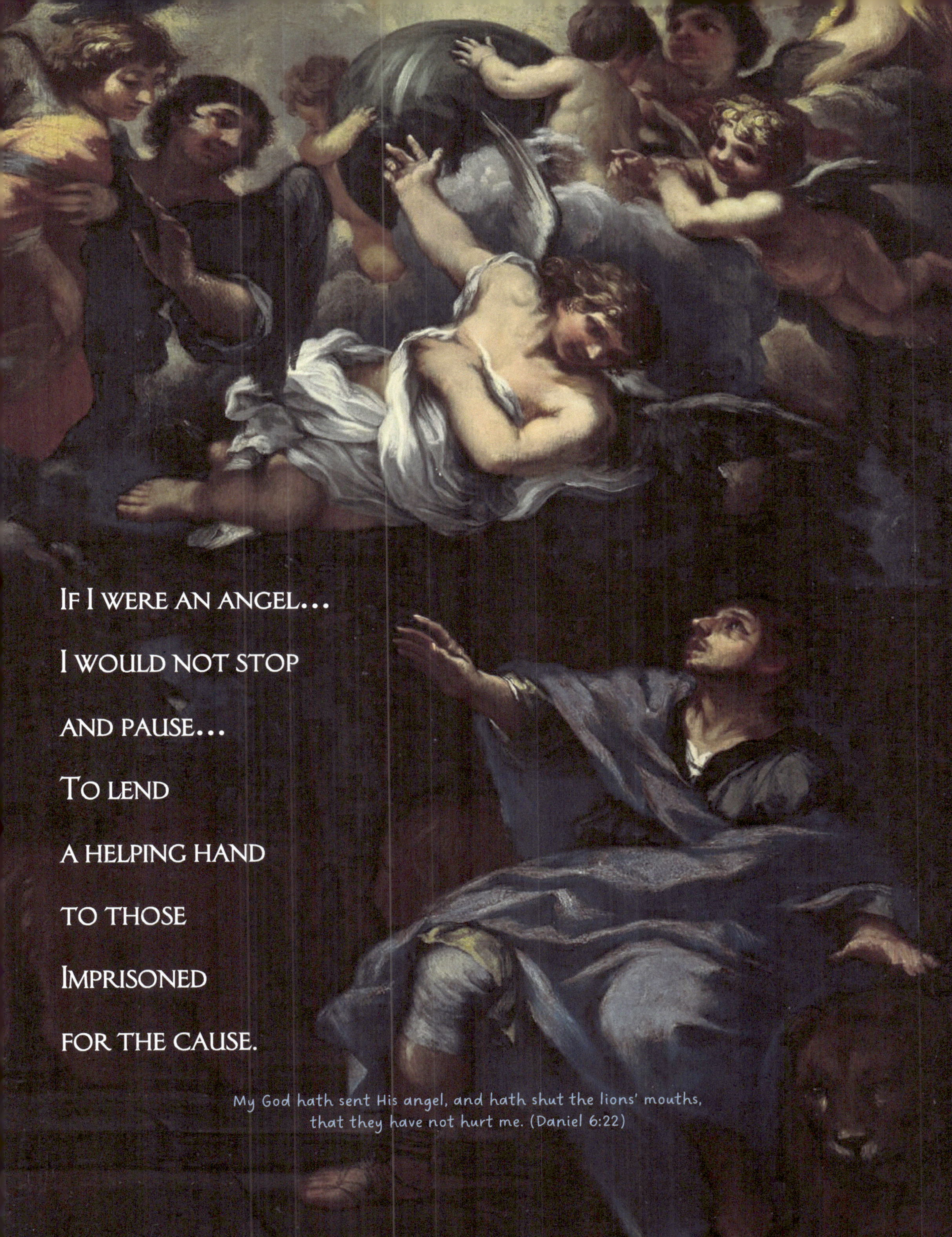
If I were an angel…
I would not stop
and pause…
To lend
a helping hand
to those
Imprisoned
for the cause.
My God hath sent His angel, and hath shut the lions' mouths,
that they have not hurt me. (Daniel 6:22)

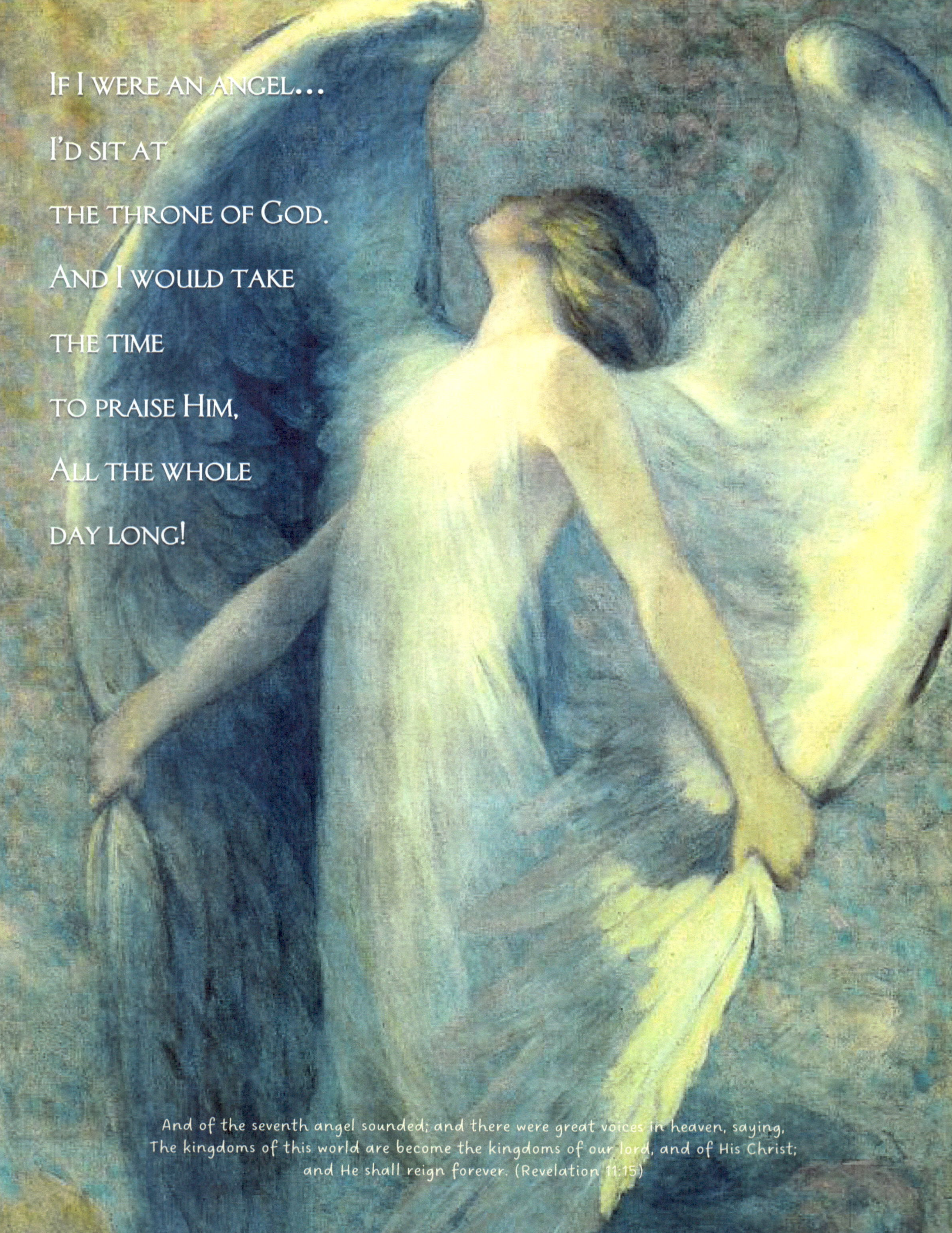
If I were an angel…
I'd sit at
the throne of God.
And I would take
the time
to praise Him,
All the whole
day long!
And of the seventh angel sounded; and there were great voices in heaven, saying,
The kingdoms of this world are become the kingdoms of our lord, and of His Christ;
and He shall reign forever. (Revelation 11:15)

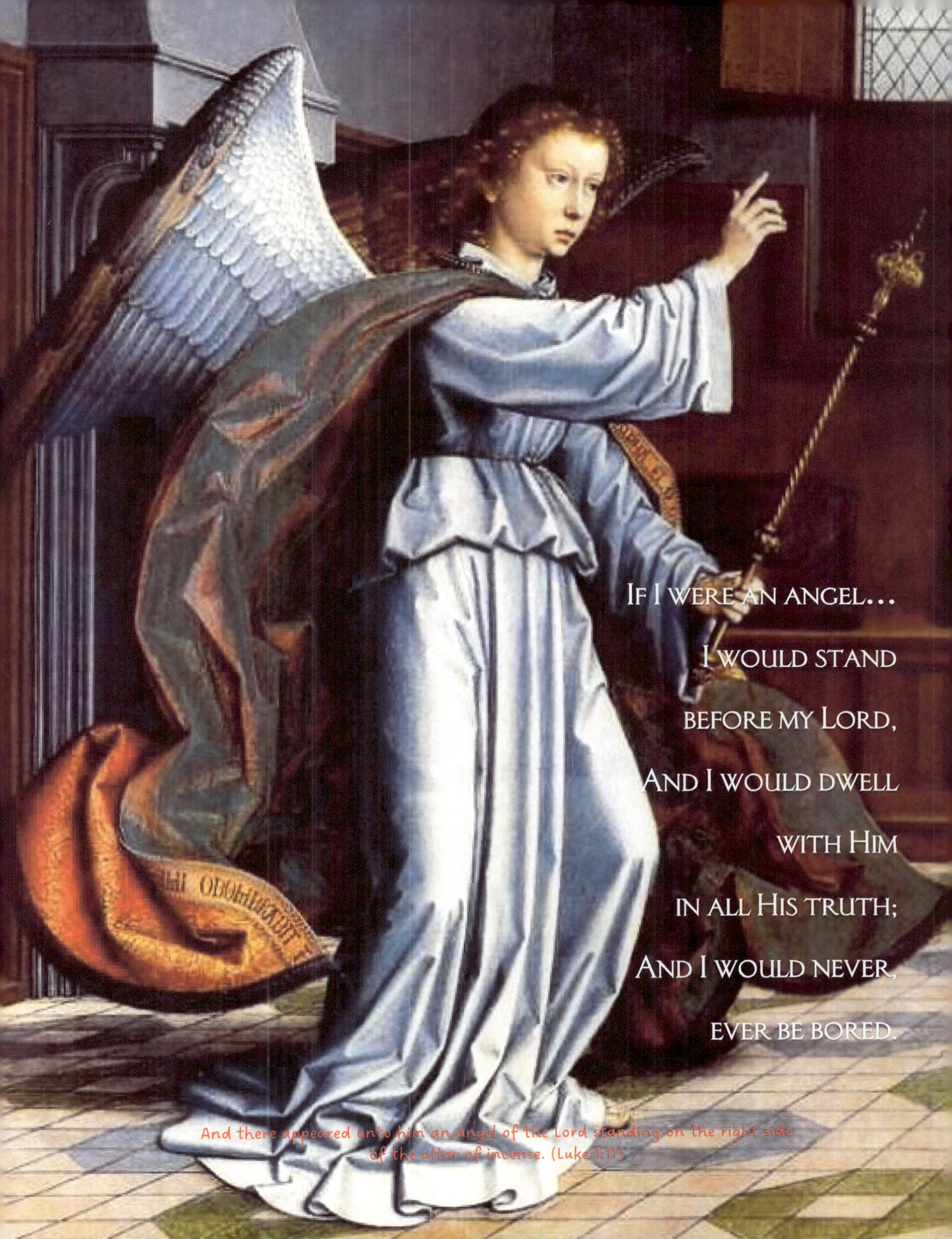
IF I WERE AN ANGEL…
I WOULD STAND
BEFORE MY LORD,
AND I WOULD DWELL
WITH HIM
IN ALL HIS TRUTH;
AND I WOULD NEVER,
EVER BE BORED.
And there appeared unto him an angel of the Lord standing on the right side
of the altar of incense. (Luke 1:11)

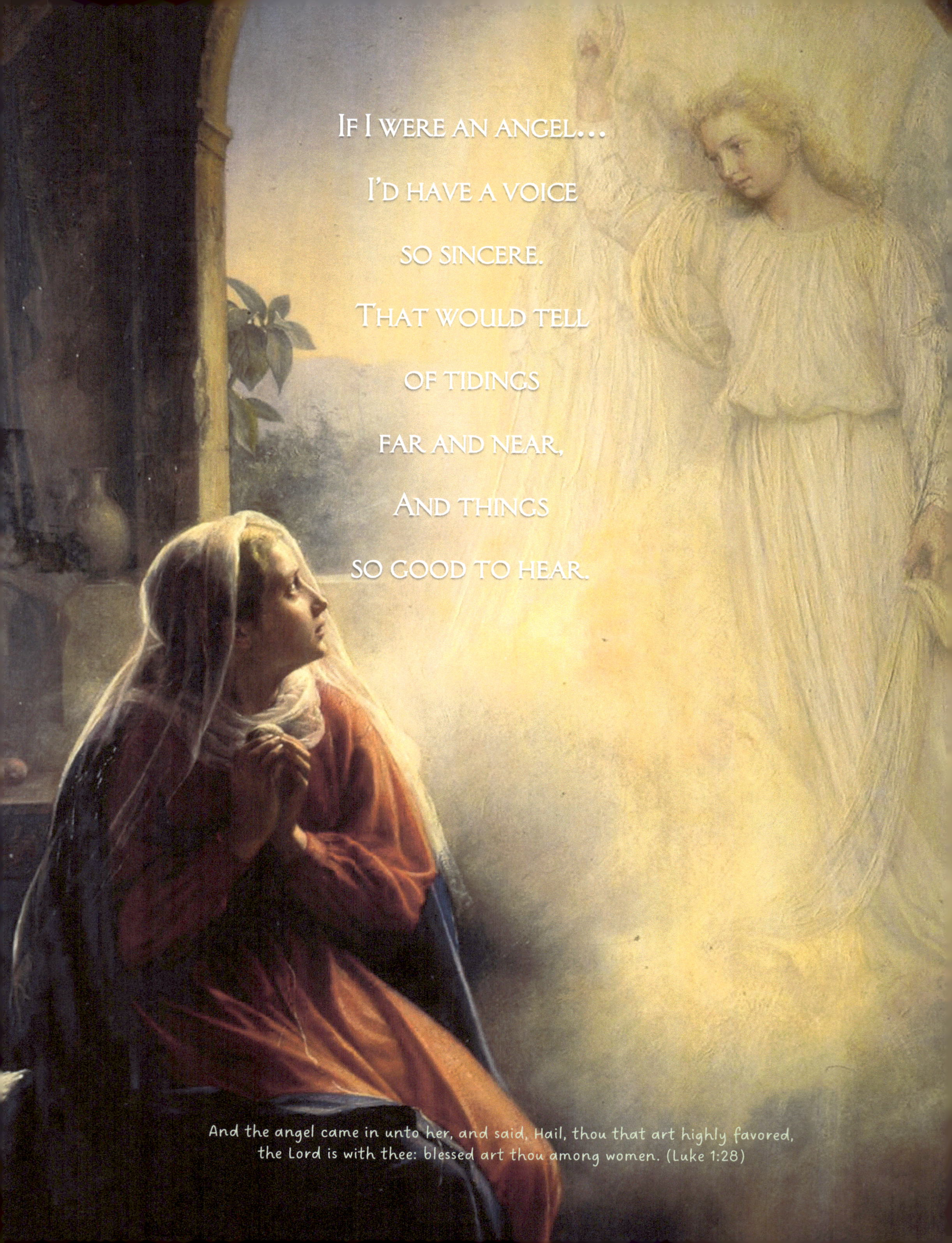

If I were an angel...

I'd have a voice

so sincere.

That would tell

of tidings

far and near,

And things

so good to hear.

And the angel came in unto her, and said, Hail, thou that art highly favored, the Lord is with thee: blessed art thou among women. (Luke 1:28)

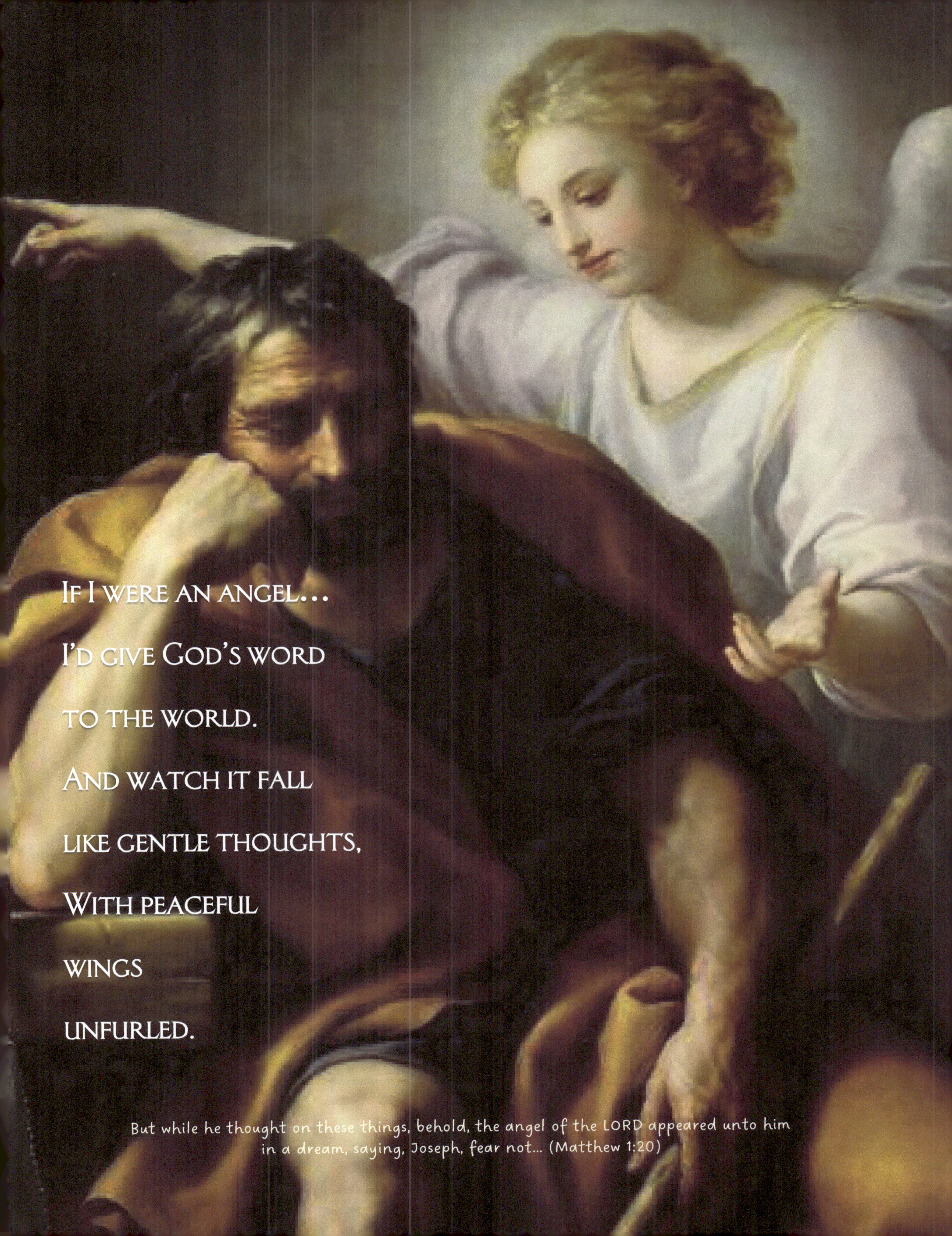

If I were an angel…

I'd give God's word

to the world.

And watch it fall

like gentle thoughts,

With peaceful

wings

unfurled.

But while he thought on these things, behold, the angel of the LORD appeared unto him
in a dream, saying, Joseph, fear not… (Matthew 1:20)

If I were an angel...

I'd tell of

God's unending love,

That he has

for all His children,

And the Spirit

He sends as a dove.

And the LORD answered the angel that talked with me with good words and comfortable words. (Zechariah 1:13)

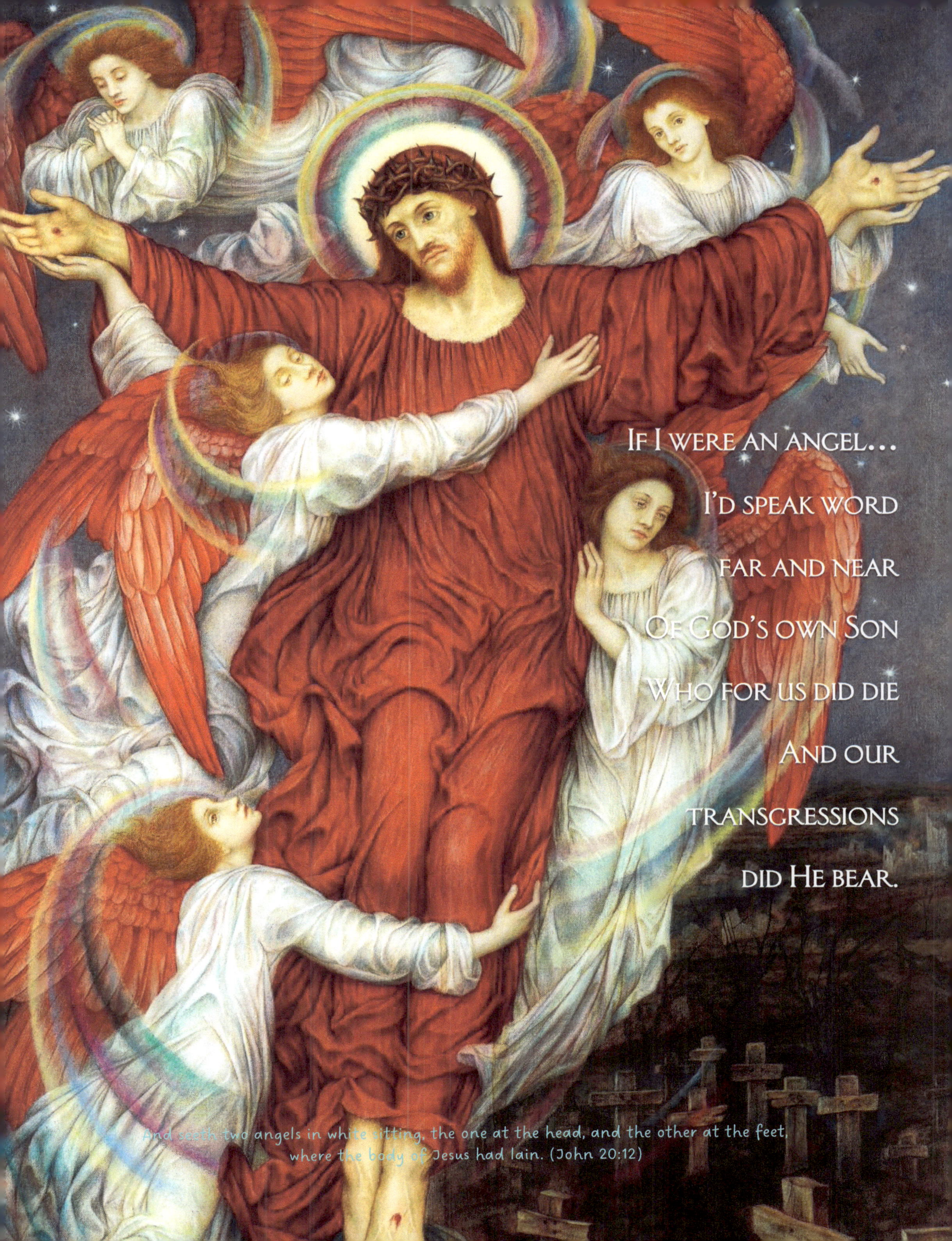
If I were an angel…
I'd speak word
far and near
Of God's own Son
Who for us did die
And our
transgressions
did He bear.
And seeth two angels in white sitting, the one at the head, and the other at the feet,
where the body of Jesus had lain. (John 20:12)

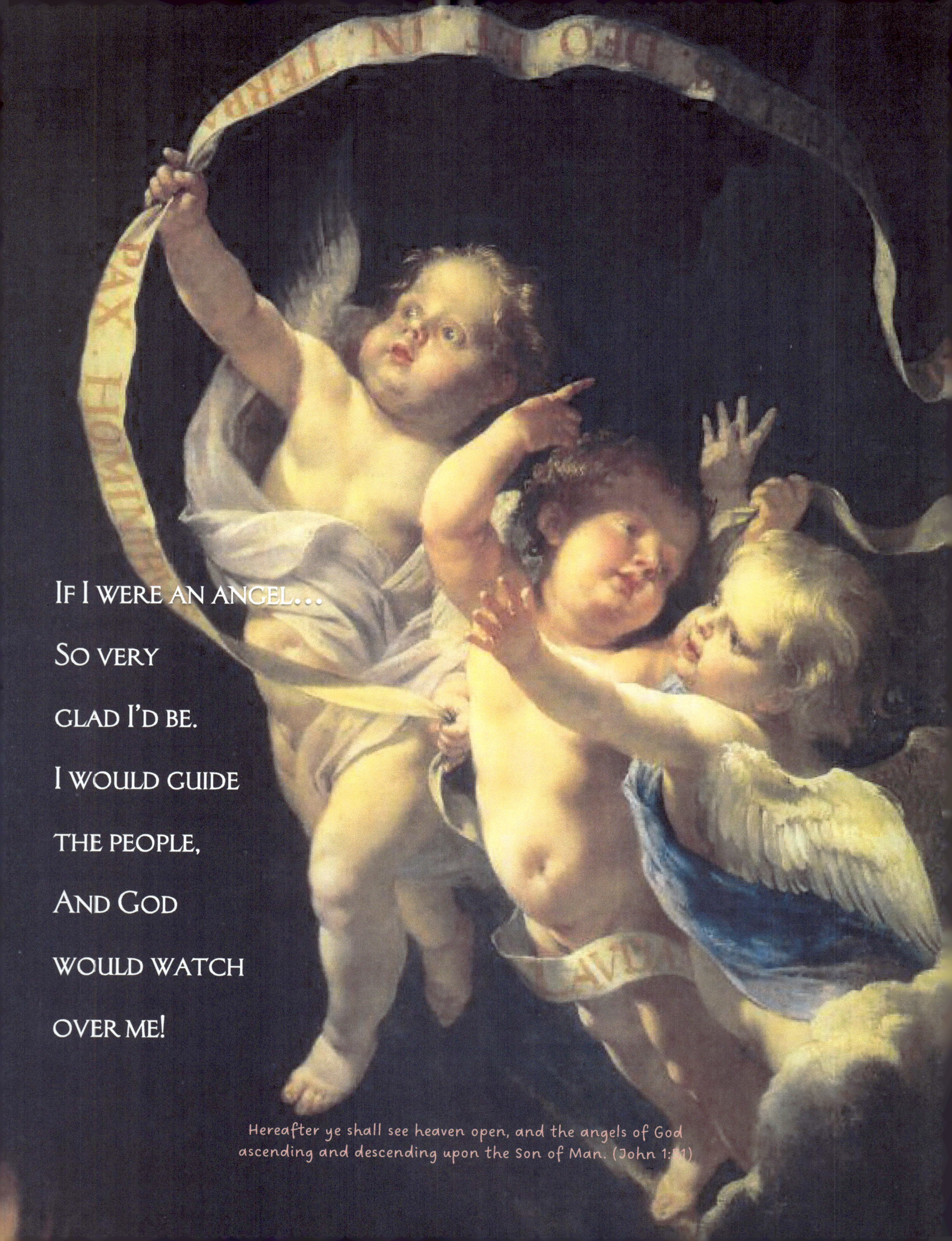

If I were an angel...

So very

glad I'd be.

I would guide

the people,

And God

would watch

over me!

Hereafter ye shall see heaven open, and the angels of God
ascending and descending upon the Son of Man. (John 1:51)

Works of Art Used In This Book

- *Vintage Angel Girls* (Unknown)
- *Music-Making Angels* (Panel 3) by Hans Memling (c. 1483-1494)
- *Angel Harp* (Unknown)
- *The Guardian Angel* by Bernardo Strozzi (c. 1630)
- *The Guardian Angel* by Wilhelm Von Kaulbach (1800s)
- *Victorian flying Angel* (Unknown)
- *An Angel Awakens the Prophet Elijah* by Juan Antonio Frias y Escalante (1667)
- *Guardian Angel Crosisng Bridge* by Hans Zatzka Zabateri (1918)
- *Tobias and the Angel* by Eduardo Rosales Gallinas (c. 1858-1863)
- *The Angel Appears to Hagar and Ishmael* by Guercino (c. 1652-1653)
- *The Annunciation – The Angel Gabriel* by Gaudenzio Ferrari (c. 1508-1509)
- *Saint Michael the Archangel* by Claudio Coello (1660s)
- *Daniel in the Lions' Den* by Berettini Pietro Detto Pietro da Cortona (c. 1657-1663)
- *The Angel* by William Baxter Closson (1912)
- *The Annunciation* by Gerard David (1520)
- *The Annunciation* by Carl Heinrich Bloch (c. before 1890)
- *The Dream of St. Joseph* by Anton Raphael Mengs (c. 1773-1774)
- *Angel de la Guardia* (Unknown)
- *The Red Cross* by Evelyn de Morgan (1914-1916)
- *Victorian Cherubs* (Unknown)
- *Raffaels Angels* by Raphael (c. 1512-1513)

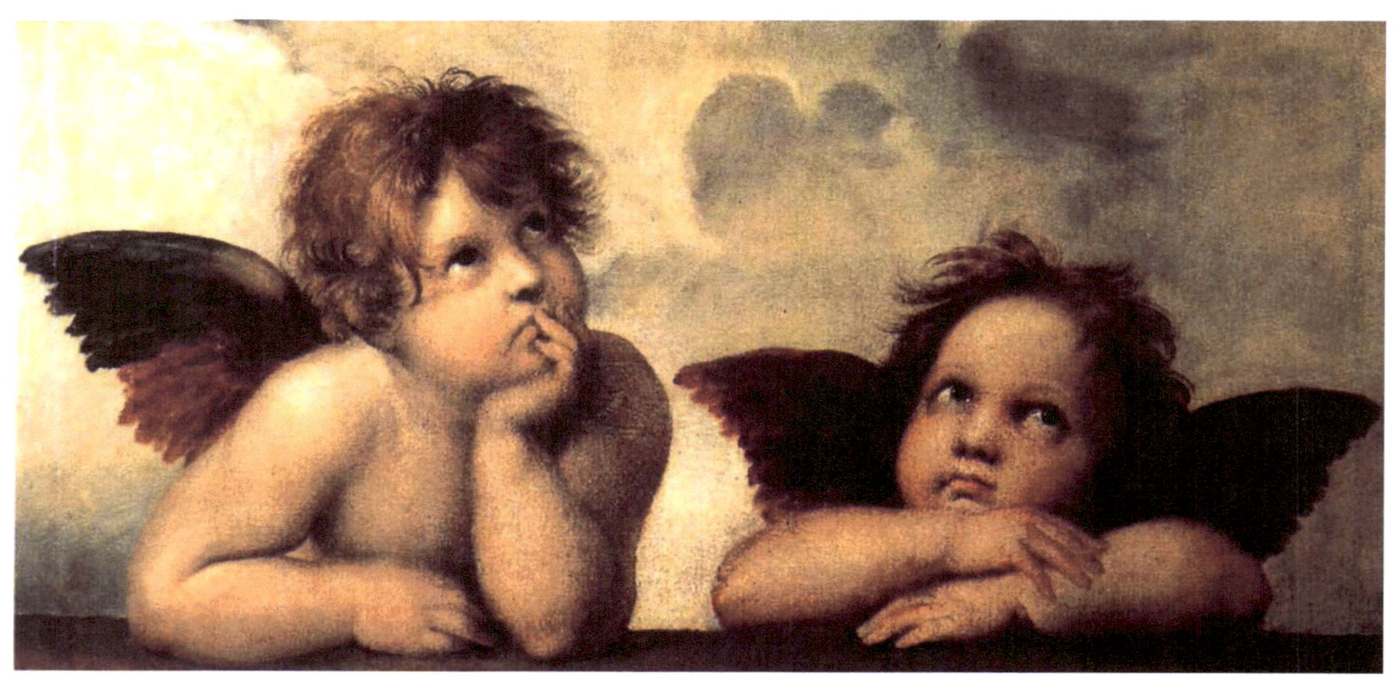

About The Author

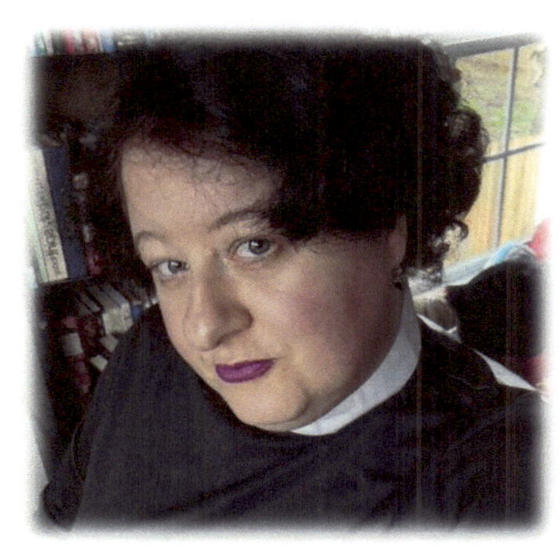

Lee Ann B. Marino, Ph.D., D.Min., D.D., is a full-time minister, author, professor, editor, and publisher. She has been involved with Christian ministry for over 25 years and serves as a licensed and ordained minister of the Gospel, serving in her own ministry, Sanctuary Apostolic Fellowship Empowerment (SAFE) Ministries. Under her ministry heading, she is founder of Sanctuary International Fellowship Tabernacle - SIFT in Charlotte, North Carolina. Within the Kingdom of God, Dr. Marino serves in the office of apostle. She works as a theologian specializing in queer and feminist theology, with concentrations in pneumatology, leadership development, Ephesians 4:11 ministry, ministry startup development, conceptual theology, and apostolic theology. She is host of the top 20 percentile *Kingdom Now* podcast and also serves as Chancellor for Apostolic Covenant Theological Seminary (ACTS).

Dr. Marino has spent nearly 30 years in Christian education, from elementary school all the way through to postgraduate education. She is proud to stand as the author of curriculum, over 35 books on various theological and spiritual topics (including five Amazon bestsellers), and as a long-time instructor and pioneer in the fields of Pentecostal Christian education, seminary, women's study, queer theology, and apostolic theological study.

Known to those she works with as spiritual mom, teacher, leader, confidant, and devoted friend, Dr. Marino continues to grow, transform, and change, receiving new teaching, revelation, and insight into this thing we call "ministry." Through years of pressing, seeking, and spiritual growth, Dr. Marino stands as herself, here to present what God has given to her for any who have an ear to hear. Her main website is www.kingdompowernow.org.

www.ingramcontent.com/pod-product-compliance
Lightning Source LLC
LaVergne TN
LVHW070207110826
845147LV00002B/527

* 9 7 8 1 9 4 0 1 9 7 7 4 6 *